PLAYS

Oct 2005

To
Dean

I taught this several years ago after attending a workshop by Sol B. River in Leeds.

I feel this belongs to you because your brother features, writes and performs in it. Thus, you belong in it too.

Love
Sharon xxx.

Sol B. River

PLAYS

MOOR MASTERPIECES
TO RAHTID
UNBROKEN

From The Agenda Album

OBERON BOOKS
LONDON

First published in 1997 by Oberon Books Ltd (incorporating Absolute Classics), 521 Caledonian Road, London, N7 9RH. Tel: 0171 607 3637 / Fax: 0171 607 3629

Copyright Sol B. River © 1997

Sol B. River is hereby identified as author of these works in accordance with Section 77 of the Copyright, Designs and Patents Act 1988. The author has asserted his moral rights.

British Library Cataloguing-in-Publication Data
A catalogue record for this book is available from the British Library.

ISBN 1 870259 82 3

Cover design: Andrzej Klimowski

Typography: Richard Doust

Printed in Great Britain by Arrowhead Books, Reading.

Contents

Acknowledgements

Markus Wiener Publishing for kind permission to use John Scott's letter and George M. Horton's *Oh Liberty* and *Slavery* from the book *Blacks in Bondage* edited by Robert S. Starobin published by Markus Wiener Publishing.

David Higham Associates for kind permission to use an extract from Dilip Hiro's book *Black British White British* published by Eyre & Spottiswoode.

Harper Collins for quotes from Jean-Paul Sartre and Frantz Fanon from *The Wretched of the Earth*.

Many thanks to G G for all her help and support.

Wisdom is the principal thing; therefore get wisdom:

and with all thy getting get understanding.

Proverbs 4.7

To my Mother,

Never before have I seen so much beauty,

and to my Father's strength.

INTRODUCTION

Often I am asked about the aesthetics of Black British theatre and my lips pout because I don't want to answer. This question is far gone; you should know the answer. I say, you are older than the world, and I turn to Jean Paul Sartre and his introduction to Frantz Fanon while at the same time flicking on the box to see images of martyrs. Progression? The word struggles out; separatism for the good of the ancestors and integration for the good of all and charity begins at home. You see my history is late, but my history is my future as is my past. Nevertheless my strength belongs to yesterday and is a contribution to tomorrow.

To Rahtid and *Moor Masterpieces* are closely related and that obviously goes beyond the fact that they were written by the same mortal. I remained during that period (and the period goes on just a little longer) one blessed, upset and cautious individual. At the time of picking up the pen and writing *Moor Masterpieces* I deemed it as my last chance; although it was my first chance and chances are few and far between. However the intention in the pen was always nothing less than serious. In my early twenties I was writing by candle light, downing the pen and disappearing into bed thinking what on earth are you going on about, but my spirit knew and so did my ancestors because it was they who guided me.

On the first performance of *Moor Masterpieces* in 1994 I remember more than one member of the audience saying I cried and later on I laughed. I remember saying God bless Tyrone Huggins who against the odds with two weeks rehearsal did what he had to do. *Moor Masterpieces* was put down before it was put up and then the same again. The piece itself knows where it stands. Larrington Walker said "Did you throw up Sol? It's as if you just threw it all up".

"Maybe" I said. But sometimes I'm sick every day. Yet, *Moor Masterpieces* remains, so far one of the most edible pieces. Even then I was more patient and relaxed.

I was to throw up again, quite a concentrated gip, with *To Rahtid* or *To Raatid*; you choose, I don't mind. It was written in the same chair as *Moor Masterpieces* but a different candle. I think that candle was taller than the first one and it flickered more; some breeze from somewhere. It was put together like a chemical solution and its ingredients were never intended to be anything but honest and explosive. I tried to offend and I wanted to but I think it was just truth in the end. I was considering all that went before and all those who gave their life for me.

I knew as soon as I began to write, I knew about *To Rahtid*. I knew about the injustice, desperation and tears and the wasted lives. Some people just don't know where heaven is. Are there two heavens?

What is theatre? I think my definition would be *To Rahtid*. As 'Time Out' said, "Angela Wynter stands defiant in the face of history". I should add, "and the future". The Guardian mentioned that I write like I'm on amphetamines. Can I add again that I might have to be on something to survive this. West Africa Times wrote, "The hush that befalls the audience at the end of performance gives testimony to its power". I would say the truth, which should always be the power. In my confusion I'll continue to create clarity.

I used *Unbroken* as an escape and a brief departure to write for a dance company.

I wanted it to be powerful; for the poetic language to be furious. I wanted a relentless narrative to execute itself in a very short space of time and I wanted it to make sense. I didn't want much. I had experimented with dance and text only once before. The major task for me was that the words of *Unbroken* absolutely encapsulate and empower the heart and mind strings of the dancer so that they in turn could transfer that feeling to the audience.

I first saw Phoenix Dance Company as a boy in 1983. I obviously never suspected that at sometime in 1997 I would be writing words for the future Phoenix to dance to. It was a surprise and a privilege. I was given a brief on women and patriarchal wisdom in the book of Proverbs. It held me at first. I had to let my thinking ferment over a time; I could not determine (and the deadline was looming) but I couldn't rush ... and then six pages in maybe seven days. The freedom in those pages turned out to be almost everything I desired whilst knowing that the piece was yet to be exalted through the dance.

> *And when one day our human kind becomes full grown it will not define itself as the sum total of the whole world's inhabitants but as the infinite of their mutual needs.*

> John-Paul Sartre. *The Wretched of the Earth.*

As part of the second generation of West Indian migrants and at the same time the descendant of kings and slaves, the hurdles I've jumped since before birth mean that as part of the human race I run the race a lap behind my oppressor for he has gained a bloody lap in front. I think that when I came to the point of realising this, my feet left the ground refusing to run with the injected so that I can float and comment waiting for this brief life like grass in the wind, looking to God as my only judge and saviour.

God bless anybody who deserves it. Never wanted to be a writer. But want has nothing to do with it, rather a duty to bear witness, contribute and survive.

Sol B. River 1997

MOOR MASTERPIECES

Foreword

Tyrone Huggins

Reading *Moor Masterpieces* for the first time was not a surprise; it was intact; it was a revelation. There was language with craft, conjugation with guile, and somewhere in the mid distance was a sound track.

The array of characters was not a surprise either. They were known to me, but only once (nearly), in that line up. This was a new play, with a strident voice, alert and uncompromising. How long would it be before the sting of compromise would be felt? In this play: not at all. It was near to me, but my journey to arrive at it would take me far. The voice that I heard most, amongst the many voices that speak in this play, was familiar. It was my own voice; I had heard it once before (nearly); never so articulate, seldom so concise. I had heard it whispered, mumbled, mouthed, confounded and living in the faces and experiences of we who wish to speak, but open our mouths to find only no voice. This is the work of the writer.

In performing *Moor Masterpieces* a dialogue ensues between character (and here is a range), and audience: recognition is the title of the dialogue: narrative is the deed of the characters. And still the sound-track plays.

As an opening to a theatre of the 'free form' *Moor Masterpieces* is a subtle door, ajar. Inside is history, commentary, characters re-examined, narrative spun like a spider's web, humour, pathos and above all people who, from moment to moment, will convince us that they see the whole story. It is only by this story's end that it becomes obvious that the sum is only the beginning of the parts. This is a play for all reasons.

Tyrone Huggins, September 1996

Characters

OTHELLO
SOLOMON
SLAVE
OLD WEST INDIAN MAN
YOUNG MAN
PRINCE OF MOROCCO
IAGO
OLD MAN

Moor Masterpieces was first presented in the Quarry theatre of The West Yorkshire Playhouse, Leeds, on 5 April, 1994, with the following cast:

OTHELLO
SOLOMON
SLAVE
OLD WEST INDIAN MAN
YOUNG MAN,   Tyrone Huggins

PRINCE OF MOROCCO (Voice Over)
IAGO (Voice Over)
OLD MAN (Voice Over),   Larrington Walker

ACT ONE

VOICE OVER: [*1]As early as 1554, John Locke, an English merchant, brought slaves to London from West Africa.

The first slave trade expedition by Sir John Hawkins armed with the Queen's charter carried a shipment of five hundred slaves from West Africa to the new world.

1770. There were eighteen thousand black slaves forming 3% of the population of London.

It was decided that there were too many Africans in England and so following the Privy Council's Act, the Queen appointed Caster Van Zeuden who was a merchant of Lubeck to transport the blackamoors out of the country.

1779. Liverpool newspaper, "To be sold by auction at George Dunbar's office on Thursday next, the 21st Inst, at one o'clock, a black boy aged about 14 years old and a large mountain tiger cat".

Masters were encouraged to free their slaves. Lord Mansfield's judgement in 1772 gave an impetus to the anti-slavery movement. But freed slaves found it impossible to find work. They became residents of the common lodging houses for destitutes in the St Giles area of London. This earned them the nickname of St Giles Blackbirds.

1786. When the government's attention was drawn to the plight of the freed slaves, its response was, "repatriate them". 411 blacks and 60 white prostitutes were bundled off to Sierra Leone to form Freetown.

1870. Britain had more or less returned to her original stage of being a purely white nation. But Britain was now an imperial nation and a lot of traffic developed between her and her colonies.

[*1] extract from *Black British White British* by Dilip Hiro published by Eyre & Spottiswode.

1680 to 1786. More than two million slaves were carried across the Atlantic and the suffering continued.

There endeth the lesson.

The stage comprises an old wooden chair that takes centre stage and a small, old wooden table upon which rests a couple of candles and a chess board. Around the stage are various games and a military game, complete with soldiers. The other games around about consist of an old medicine ball and a croquet set. The stage is dimly lit – maybe in amber and completely littered with rubbish of white screwed up paper. Before the actor's entrance and before the audience are fully seated, Terence Trent D'arby's, "Succumb to Me" plays the audience in followed by "Save This Promised Land" by Des'ree from beginning to end. Near the end of the track, SOLOMON enters from stage right. He wears a purple robe and drinks from a gold cup and takes his seat at the chess table and then assumes a thinking position.

VOICE OVER: And God gave Solomon wisdom and understanding beyond measure and largeness of mind like the sand on the seashore, so that Solomon's wisdom surpassed the wisdom of all the people of the east and all the wisdom of Egypt for he was wiser than all other men.

Light up as SOLOMON gets down on his knees to pray.

SOLOMON: O Lord, thou hast searched me and known me
Thou knowest my downsitting and mine uprising
Thou understandeth my thoughts afar off
Thou compassest my path and my lying down,
And art acquainted with all my ways
For there is not a word in my tongue, but lo,
O Lord thou knowest it altogether
Thou has beset me behind and before,
And laid thine hand upon me
Such knowledge is too wonderful for me,
It is high. I cannot attain to it

SOLOMON rises to his feet and addresses the audience.

I am the preacher. Solomon, the son of David. I said to myself. I have acquired great wisdom surpassing all who were over Jerusalem before me and my mind has had great experience of wisdom and knowledge. And I applied my mind to know wisdom and to know madness and folly. I perceived that this is but a striving after the wind. For in much wisdom is much vexation, and he who increases knowledge increases sorrow ... Vanity of vanities, vanity of vanities! ... All is vanity!

So I turned to consider wisdom and madness and folly for what can the man do who comes after the king, only what he has already done? Then I saw that wisdom excels folly as light excels darkness but I saw one fate come to all of them. Then I said to myself what befalls the fowl will befall me also. Why then have I been so very wise? All this is vanity and a striving after the wind.

Why then has man suppressed so many of his fellow men, saturated in hate and jealousy and prejudice rising from dust and returning to the same? It is so very sad that great men have to die and poor men want to destroy them.

I, being me, was allowed to see, like Othello before me. Although he is me and I he, ... the great leaders of my kind, all black and comely, and each time I ask these men what will deliver the Moor of the 21st century? They all answered the same. An exodus, a return, in mind and body, physically or mentally to that place all Moors should go. I asked again, my words pointed in no particular direction because I could never determine from whereabouts the answer would arrive. I, although the biggest in stature and wisdom, had no choice but to respect these men, and God had allocated to them their own space. Occasionally we would meet and talk. Whenever such an event takes place the elements shudder, the sun often hides itself and stars fall to earth. It is funny and strange to me. I saw them before they were them but after they became who they were to become they never stopped being ... never. And they left instruction for future Moors to follow. All I can do is watch as the instruction is ignored ... How long wilt thou sleep? O sluggard? When wilt thou arise out of thy sleep? Yet a little sleep, a little slumber, a little folding of the hand to sleep. So shall they poverty come as one that travelleth and they want as an armed man. Every time one of these men were born Heaven cried!

All men should know that you will pay tomorrow for what you have done today. Because these men, all these great men did just that. Who are they, you ask. Who are these men! Whoever you are, come forth!

ACT TWO

Scene 1

Military drums start to play. SOLOMON changes his purple robe for a military cloak. He makes moves on the board games.

OTHELLO: One fine day in the middle of the night
Two dead men got up to fight
Two blind men to see the fun
One dumb man to shout hurrah
A paralysed donkey was passing by
Kick the blind man in his eye
Kicked him through a nine inch wall
And drowned him in a dry foot pan

He knocks over the pieces on the board with one swipe of his right hand

I am around 1604. They spelt it O.T.H.E.L.L.O. It is I, the Moor, or so they say, released from prison but for a day. You see a thousand years is like a day in God's sight and I am his afternoon delight. Thus I live for ever and a day, drawing in all life's experience along the way, from Garvey to Selassie to Mandela I've seen and I come before, after and in between.

OTHELLO gets up from his seat and proceeds to play around with the chess board and the military game at the same time.

Welcome aboard the good ship Othello! That's he that was Othello? Here I am. But I have to question my existence, my very being. How and why in 1602. I performed to an adoring and bemused audience, I do not know. They wanted to see me as an evil mass come to take their fair daughter. The spectators were ready to adopt her and banish me. The story of my life. The dark person in the dark part.

VO/ IAGO: O beware my lord of jealousy! It is the green
eyed monster which doth mock the meat it feeds on. That
cuckold lives in bliss who, certain of his fate, loves not his
wronger, but O, what damned minutes tells he o'er who
dotes, yet doubts – suspects, yet fondly loves!

OTHELLO: O misery!

Is that how all this is to be, because now I know, I could see
the future even then, but could not help being led into the
trap like the slaves of Africa that came before and after me.
And although a mighty warrior I am, I could not fight all
men and even if I could how could I neglect my own heart?
I gave it, my heart, my all to Desdemona, the fairest of
maidens, it was her or a Nubian Princess and Nubian
Princess, those two words, have haunted me ever since.
Whom am I to blame? Not God. He has protected me, no,
who? I, throughout all my wars, have taken charge of my
own mind and so I have had to decide on strategy and
manoeuvres of all kinds, and decisions in war have to be
sure! ... But as for the mind that makes decisions for me in
peace and my peace I thought was Desdemona, but not
even she knew the pain that chased me around my own
mind. I should say that I'm deep enough to know that shade
is irrelevant, but I'm shallow enough to know that it is
irrelevant. But let me ask you, is it better to be deep or
shallow? I still ask this question of myself and have
concluded on circumstance and saturation of mind and
geography. Even before I was fooled by the evil of my cast
and my own warrior like thinking. Let me see, how many
people did I have to convince other than my lover, how
quickly did the rot set in? I tell you even before I was
conceived they hated me. Like worms of a strange and
strong kind, laborious they were not. And so I regret all but
God because I trusted him to keep me and he has. My mind
altered quickly after my departure from life apart from the
obvious spiritual transition and metamorphosis. I met
(*Pause.*) I was allowed to meet so many victors from before
and after me and because of the grace, the pure grace of

God ... I was even allowed to become some of them for a time. And so the decision that haunted me for so long does no longer, because I gave up the ghost to take another. And as I wonder I feel a fulfilment vested in few. My fellow men, my peers, Moors like me, I am set now to consult and protect. And so in a way even like Iago I can become thus or thus as God would allow me but all within the spheres of good.

VO/PRINCE OF MOROCCO: I was not protected

OTHELLO: Who?

VO/PRINCE OF MOROCCO: I

OTHELLO: I mean who!

VO/PRINCE OF MOROCCO: The Prince of Morocco. I overheard your speech. Your words travel far. I am envious.

OTHELLO: Why?

VO/PRINCE OF MOROCCO: Not only did you secure a much larger role than I, you also have ended up somewhere near the right hand of God. I watched your battle with the cast, and during which I took a handkerchief to my brow ... no pun intended.

I mean at least you won the maiden, but how is it that you lost her and in the same mix lost yourself?

OTHELLO: Why, look you now. How unworthy a thing you make of me! You would play upon me, you would seem to know my stops. You would pluck out the heart of my mystery. You would sound me from my lowest note to the top of my compass; and there is much music, excellent voice in this little organ. Yet cannot you make it speak. 'Sblood do you think I am easier to be played on than a pipe? Call me what instrument you will, though you can fret me, you cannot play upon me ... Hamlet I know him ... so well ... and you I know also, better than you know yourself.

Was I lost before you? Whereabouts lay your destiny that your fate, such a fate in which you depended so much, lay within a casket?

VO/PRINCE OF MOROCCO: I took my chance, as you did.

OTHELLO: It is an unfair comparison for simply because my chores were far more varied than yours. It would be hard to compare my pain to your foolish and shallow acts. Sweeping in and out like so much nonsense. Just a mention from a well wisher. Not to look upon the wine when it stains the glass would have been a good instruction.

VO/PRINCE OF MOROCCO: I secured a role, not the bottle.

OTHELLO: And your fate, even your first words on meeting Portia were flimsy and sad. Mislike me not for my complexion. You were never even going to get the opportunity to go where I went. You should have stayed within the boundaries of Morocco.

VO/PRINCE OF MOROCCO: May I ask a simple question?

OTHELLO: Shoot

VO/PRINCE OF MOROCCO: How did you come by the part of Othello?

OTHELLO: I had heard of a man by the name of Shakespeare, a great playwright amongst other things, so I took him some of my best writing so that he could give it his evaluation.

VO/PRINCE OF MOROCCO: What did he say?

OTHELLO: He said, "you're black".

VO/PRINCE OF MOROCCO: How did you reply?

OTHELLO: I looked at myself in a nearby mirror and said, "yes, I am".

VO/PRINCE OF MOROCCO: Then what?

OTHELLO: He showed great interest in my work, brought me a slice of bread and some beer and suggested that I enable him to make some changes. "But I am the star", I said, "and a very noble man". "I have indeed returned from fighting wars for true". "That may be so", he said, "but Moor you are and Moor you shall remain". "That is true", I replied, "I wish to be none other". "Good", he said, "but if you are to work with me you must recognise me as the master".

So I worked with him, to my detriment. Othello I may have been, but the act and the whole task, by the time he had finished with my story had driven me almost to madness. And eventually all the way to madness, so that I killed the female thesp and then myself. Some success is all I wanted to find, but Europe struck and killed me from both in front and behind.

VO/PRINCE OF MOROCCO: Don't you believe in a free spirit, and that love is stronger than hate?

OTHELLO: What love?! You asked for the fairest maiden northward bound. It could have been anybody, you just wanted anyone fair.

You see my prince, our root, our course, had already been set.

If you or I could have seen the plans then maybe we could have asked God to consult the elements and have them bid come, join our side. But God helps those who help themselves and I was tempted to ask him if he loved me like he said he did. (*Looks about.*) Now do you love me like you said you did?! Because of the suffering that concerned itself with my mind I knew that until I crossed that river, the river known as life, I would not be satisfied and I knew that.

The pure complexity of life, the very fact that Shakespeare would take me for a tragedy was known before I was born, he had that power. So yes, as Solomon says, and I decided it was a striving after the wind, the new era I waited for. The crossing of the river because my life had been preordained. For those who come after me, take me as an example for nothing but an Exodus, a return in mind and body, physically or mentally, you choose, because to that place all Moors should consider.

OTHELLO tosses a coin.

Which side?

VO/PRINCE OF MOROCCO: Heads

OTHELLO: Tails. Pick again.

VO/PRINCE OF MOROCCO: Heads

OTHELLO: Tails again.

VO/PRINCE OF MOROCCO: Heads again

OTHELLO: Tails

VO/PRINCE OF MOROCCO: Heads again

OTHELLO: Spare me. But tell me, if I were to toss this coin a thousand times and it were to land on tails every time, what would that suggest?

VO/PRINCE OF MOROCCO: A fault

OTHELLO: Damn right it would! A conspiracy. You can't win. The inscription on the casket read, in hope that you would win your fairest creature, who chooseth me shall gain what many men desire, and you in your foolish haste shouted come, bring me unto my chance.

VO/PRINCE OF MOROCCO: We all have to take chances.

OTHELLO: Have you been as wise as bold? Thus losers depart. You, like I, was only a guest. Guest, ever only a guest.

VO/PRINCE OF MOROCCO: I thought that it was fine for the heart to rule the mind. I was taken over, greatly infatuated. I apologise Othello, if my actions seemed untoward.

OTHELLO: They promise freedom, but they themselves are slaves of corruption. For whatever overcomes a man to that he is enslaved.

OTHELLO tosses the coin again.

Which side?

VO/PRINCE OF MOROCCO: Heads

OTHELLO: Heads it is. And so, infatuated a Moor should not be. Instead his own life and destiny he should take care of and uphold. It is imperative that he understands the basics of the economy and having said that his own mind must be structured and composed to the extent that he understands the beginning of wisdom, which is to get insight. I whisper now into the ears of my brothers, choose your love wisely, choose, but choose wisely, let your manner be close to God.

OTHELLO tosses the coin

Which side?

VO/PRINCE OF MOROCCO: Heads

OTHELLO: That it is, twice right

Fade out. OTHELLO takes his seat.

Scene 2

Music in the background and we hear the sound effect of wind. All papers lying on the stage are blown around and about. Lights go down to a very low dim and a surreal type spot light is placed on SOLOMON. Smoke blows onto the stage. Another spot is placed opposite him so that during the course of this next monologue, every time he mentions a name the spot is cast onto an alternative spot.

SOLOMON: Do not worry. If you cannot connect things from the past to the things of the present, things from the past are things of the future ... and they all connect.

I had witnessed all these great men during their time on earth. I watched the people who followed and shook my head at all those that ignored them.

They stand before me now cognate to a light. I can see such men as Benjamin Banneker – mathematician, inventor, surveyor, philosopher and abolitionist. In front of him I saw William Du Bois, standing next to Booker T Washington. At the back mine eyes focused in on a strange looking man. When I had stared for too long he called out "Jean Da Sable – founder of Chicago, Illinois 1774!" This was a moment in love, for sitting not ten metres away was Edmonia Lewis, 1845 to 1890 sculpting with clay and a piece at her feet named forever free.

I heard music and as my left ear twitched I turned in that direction. (*Music starts soft piano.*) To my delight it was Samuel Coleridge Taylor playing the Hiawatha and. George M. Horton whispering poetry. Adjacent Duke Ellington sat playing ... simply vivacious. People, all Moors, so many stood before me in their ghostly form. Langston Hughes stepped forward and recited his poem to me ... "I've known rivers, I've known rivers ancient as the world and older than the flow of human blood in human veins. My soul has grown deep like rivers" ... and then he stepped back.

As I swung my head to and fro, the greatness kindled my soul. Every great Moor from Paul Robeson to James Baldwin to Elaine Locke. A plump man stepped forward and announced, "If you have not confidence in self you are twice defeated in the race of life. With confidence, you have won even before you have started". He held a model in his hand of the Black Star Line, one of a fleet of steamships. I remember the time he convinced his people to board them.

Then I recognised a controversial man with glasses and a goatee beard and another beside him. The three of them stepped forward and I recognised them as Marcus Garvey, Malcolm X and Martin Luther King. I said, "how?" And they said, "we don't know". And then a tear became visible in all our eyes and we looked at each other and said, "too much pain, too much hurt, why has man done this to us and himself. Why is man so inhumane?"

As I looked these men up and down they did the same, I had a picture in my own mind of people dismissing the anger and the pain, waving the hurt away. Mr King stepped onto a box and said again, "If man doesn't put an end to war, war will put an end to mankind". My chest felt tight and I turned back as if looking in the direction of my maker, and I looked deep into myself. Then Malcolm said, "I would welcome an opportunity to defend anything you ever heard me say to anyone, anywhere, at any time". Then again I saw more figures emerging, from Arthur Ash to Haile Selassie and Othello appeared at my left side and said, "I have been speaking with Dr King. You know, I don't fear anybody". I nodded my head ... "Yes, never fear anyone". Toussaint Louverture turned his head towards me and smiled.

And for the last time I was allowed to see again. First the dead, before their resurrection, the murdered, they numbered like grains of sand, faces of slaves, faces of martyrs, faces of modern leaders, faces of pain and faces of people just ordinary people. (*Starts to remove the top half of his clothing, stretching out his arms.*) The amount of faces alone was incredible. Soldiers, sailors, brothers and sisters. But they all looked like angels. And all like me, all the same shade as me, all this glorious shade!

SOLOMON collapses into himself and cries and then falls to the ground as if asleep. Fade to black.

ACT THREE

Music plays while SOLOMON is reciting his poem. In the darkness he begins to place chains on his ankles and wrists. He strips down to his loins and calmly places the chains on his body.

SLAVE: Then I saw and considered it
I looked and received instruction
A little sleep, a little slumber
A little folding of the hands to rest
And poverty will come upon you like a robber
And want like an armed man

Extract from Sam Cooke's "Change Gonne Come" as the slave sits at the table. A candle is lit and he begins to write. As the song fades out the SLAVE picks up his writing paper to the candle light and begins to read what he has written. He has a slight African / American accent for the duration of this act.

SLAVE: [2]Dear Sir, I wish to inform you that it has been our great and long desire to go to Liberia for a settlement but we could not comply with our wishes on account of not being free at first. Since that time our master promised to set us free at his death, at which time we expected to obtain our freedom and our master, old Mr John Enders, has died very near 2 years ago at which time our freedom was talk about by white gentlemen of this city, and at this time young Mr John Enders, son of the deceased, said to us be not troubled for he would do all for us that his father had said in the Will and that we were then working for ourselves, and since that time we have been kept here in bondage, and hire out by the year, and do not get the money that we are hire out for, and we has said and done everything in our power to get our rights according to the Will of old master, but being slaves we has not obtain them as yet, and this is the reason you has not heard from

[2] John Scott's Letter from *Blacks In Bondage,* edited by Robert S. Starobin, published by Markus Wiener Publishing.

us and the reason why we are kept so long from the home of our forefathers in Africa. There is now about 118 in all who has been left free, and we humbly beg you to help us out if you can, if you can undertake for us and advocate our cause we shall be very glad for you to do so, or if you can give us any advice or information how we should act in regard to this matter it will be thankfully received, and you will be rewarded. We have made some 2 or 3 attempts by lawyers to get a copy of the Will, but they have deceived us and got our money, and we are left to grope our way in bondage, far from Africa, the home of our forefathers. Our desire for going to Liberia was on the increase up to last July 19th and they are still on the increase up to this present moment. It was on the 18th of last July that a number of us went to the court house, to the clerk's office, to hear the Will of our master read, but the officers send us away with a admonition to be still on the subject, but we cannot be still until we get home to Africa. Out of 118 slaves there is some 45 or 50 of them who can read, and some 6 or 7 who can read and write and one is a very good preacher and most of us have free wives with many boy children. Dear sir, you will please send us as many pamphlets as you can spare at present and when you answer this you will then write us word what the pamphlets will cost us. The whole of this matter to some extent has gotten out in the public and if you wish to see some of the newspapers of last July the 19th and 20th dates, we will try to send you some as soon as they are wrote for. Our bribed lawyers has gotten some 2 or 3 copy for us, and one of them seem to contradicts the other, which lead us to think more strongly that we were set free by our good old master, Mr John Enders. I will now close my remarks by requesting you give us an answer as soon as you can. Yours most truly, John Scott.

SLAVE puts the letter down and stands up from the table violently, breathing heavily all the time.

They won't even reply!

O God have mercy! See my desperation.

SLAVE now walks to and fro.

[3]Alas! And am I born for this?
To wear this slavish chain
Deprived of all created bliss
Through hardship, toil and pain!

How long have I in bondage lain
And languished to be free?
Alas! And must I still complain, deprived of liberty

Oh Heaven! And is there no relief?
This side the silent grave
To soothe the pain, to quell the grief
And anguish of a slave

Come liberty, thou cheerful sound
Roll through my ravished ears!
Come, let my grief in joys be drowned
And drive away my fears

Say unto foul oppression cease
Ye tyrants rage no more
And let the joyful trump of peace
Now bid the vassal soar

Soar on the pinions of that dove
Which long has cooed for thee
And breathed her notes from Africa's grave
The sound of liberty

Oh liberty! Thou golden prize
So often sought by blood
We crave thy sacred sun to rise
The gift of nature's God!

Bid slavery hid her haggard face
And barbarism fly

[3] *Oh Liberty and Slavery* by George M. Horton – from *Blacks in Bondage.*

I scorn to see the sad disgrace
In which enslaved I lie

Dear liberty! Upon thy breast
I languish to respire
And like the swan unto her nest
I'd to thy smiles retire

Oh blest asylum, heavenly balm!
Unto thy boughs I flee
And in thy shades the storm shall calm
With songs of liberty!

Release me!

He releases himself from the chains.

It was a clear day, a day that I could never forget. All our people were gone out to their work as usual and only I and my dear brother were left to mind the house. Then I saw the figures of four men vault our walls. They held us tight and placed their hands over our mouths we did not know what was happening. Our screams were stopped by a sequence of rough hands, we were separated. My heart fell to the lowest point of my body. These men, pale and dirty in colour, spat on me and ripped away my garment. Then they placed me in a coffle along with thirty to forty other slaves including women and children and then proceeded to whip me every twenty or so steps.

Next a trip on a large ship with some of my own people, even my own people guiding the slaves traders at the shore. We were packed on this ship and there my eyes witnessed things that would cause the heart to stop. I prayed that mine would. Women raped, men raped too. Diseases, and in the middle of the crossing I was kept chained to a dead man for three days before they tossed him into the sea along with one that was still alive. Unfed and unclean for days. Arriving on the

Atlantic coast I witnessed gangs of faces, their complexions too differing from ours, their string hair and the language they spoke ... I prayed to the ancestors that I would die soon if they didn't give me the strength to rise above it. And I knew that from now on, seeing all my fellow men in a strange land that only an exodus, a return in mind and body, physically and mentally, to that place we should go before it's too late.

Fade out.

ACT FOUR

Music comes in – old Jamaican track The Cha Cha Cha. The SLAVE changes into a single breasted suit, white shirt and a thin tie – everything 50's style. The OLD MAN has a pack of dominoes and a glass of punch. From here on the actor speaks in a Jamaican accent and dialect.

OLD MAN: It was 59 when I arrive in England. The so call mother country. I left my wife and one child behind. I came here at an invitation and since we had learnt so much about England in school and my older brother had served over here in the armed services during de second world war, I was happy and excited to come and fine work. It was all de craze.

Palisadoes Airport, Jamaica, my father did pay for my flight. On arriving in London, my first thoughts when I did see de, erm, buildings with smoke coming out of the top, was, what a lot of factories dem have. It was erm, later that I did find out that it was de houses the people dem live in.

Slams down a domino.

Anyway, my brother met me and did take me up a road, Grey Road, Shepherds Bush, where all de houses did look the same.

"Dis is it", im say. When I looked around me I didn't have enough room to swing a cat, as de English say.

Laughs. Slams down a domino.

One small room, we had to cook, eat, sleep and wash all in the same room for £2 a week. I did tink to myself even den, why did I leave home? I remember on my firs morning in England the cold woke me out of me sleep and so my brother lit the paraffin heater, but I couldn't stand the smell. So I decided that I would go to the exchange and see what they had for me. I'm a skilled cabinet maker me first job was outside, but it was so cold me hand couldn't even hold the hammer. So I lit a fire because I can't get warm. As soon as my boss saw it, he gave me my cards. I lasted one day. Well dis was it. The mother country got me in all kinds of trouble.

Laughs. Slams down a domino.

I wrote me wife han I sen for her to come over and bring the child. At first she didn't want to. She had heard stories about England but I had found a job that wasn't so cold and was sending money home and so eventually my wife came with me daughter. She get so big, me wife sister came too. We all stayed in the same room, so I had to start looking for a bigger place. It was difficult because so many of the houses had signs saying, "No Blacks, No Dogs, No Irish".

Me wife, complained non stop. She had a good job in Jamaica working as a teacher but nobody wanted to know that she was a teacher here. It different here her friends said, and it was.

During my first years in dis country I was insulted by de white people. Dem did ask me to do everyting from show dem me tail to asking me what it was like to live in a house compared wid a tree.

Slams down a domino.

But after a while I get used to it, even the teddy boys dem, they was de skin heads of the 50's. I did have a run in with one and two of dem.

After around two years my wife had had enough. She was quite a proud woman and said she wasn't going to work in a launderette or catering or auxiliary when she was a qualified teacher. I suppose she was right, she's a very clever woman, dat why I did marry her. She did left me and took the child with her. I tried to be strong. She didn't know how much I did want her to stay, but she did leave.

I had made a decision to come to England and I thought I should stay for a bit longer. But I will never forget what she said. She said from the time that I'm a teacher and these white people don't want me to teach dem anyting. Like dem know everything and yet them is asking me for my tail. She said that the black people here were going to be lost and only an exodus, a return in mind and body, erm, arrrr, physically or arrrr, mentally, to dat place all black people will have to go.

After she did leave, I spent a lot more time wid my brother but he died not long after. I was on my own, I did tink about going home, but I never got roun to it.

Slams down a domino.

I did start a club with some frien so we could have some kind of community. And I read a lot and widin about ten years I was foreman at my firm. The first black foreman and later union representative.

Occasionally my wife would write with a picture of my daughter, each time a little bigger, she still had not married because we still hadn't got divorce. I hadmire her so much but I understan.

I blame England for a lot of tings, but I blame myself as well, because when I look it's my choice, but when I look again I didn't have much choice. I first tink for a time my people lost all sense of self and I tink me know me did, and as soon as me realise we didn't know what to do, dem did trap us, so I tink the only ting we could hold onto was our identity or accent, our memories, and give our children a good foundation. But beyon that now, we'll woop dem at cricket as well.

Laughs. Slams down a domino.

I never miss a match

Picks up book and reads a poem.

Englan challenge W.I. to a match
Englan get catch, an run get snatch
Terror in de bowler's gaze
Bowl de ball high in a dem face
Man drop pon de grown
Englan fall down
Dutty water can put out fire
W.I. stan up straight
Bowl de ball straight to de gate

Duppy know who fi frighten
We run tings, tings no run we
Don of cricket, jussa bad bad bad
W.I. catch an snatch
Hit de ball for four, six and den more

De country colonisation
Don't stop dem determination
Englan have any an any excuse
But at de end of de day W.I. have de juice

Laughs to himself. Slams down another domino. Then he lifts up a glass of Jamaican punch.

Cheers! A few eggs, Guinness, rum, condensed milk and don't forget the nutmeg.

You can see you gotta stay strong. Don't let anybody pull you down. I know there is a lot of confusion but I held on to my identity, I know the kids have it hard because of all dis tokenism and two face attitude. I know the white man and I watch him carefully because I know he's watching me. I have learnt a lot and if I could live again in a younger body de progress would be twice as fast. Let me tell you someting. It's about the mind and realisation.

Fade out. The OLD MAN takes off his suit to reveal T-shirt and jogging bottoms along with trainers. This represents an inner city look. The actor is now an inner city kid and proceeds to vent his grievances.

YOUNG MAN: They fooled my mother. They fooled my
father. They said come to the mother country. We are a
commonwealth. Everybody's equal.

Well it's a good job that the white man is not the yardstick
by which I measure equality by, as a friend once said,
otherwise we would be fooled. I don't, I can't figure this
out. I listen to my parents talk about Jamaica every single
day and I wonder what they're doing here. Born and bred
to rahtid only to be told I don't belong. "Don't let it get
you down", mother says. "That's what the English are like,
give them as good as you get", Daddy says. So either I
chill in the ghetto feeling sorry for myself and I got the
most right. Or I act up to the white man, get a warped
education, brainwashed, conform and join the game of 2.2,
bounty life, deceiving myself, selling out or selling myself
short. Which one?

But what if I don't want to do neither!? What if the only
thing I want to do is sit here and think? Is this society
going to allow me to do that? I don't think so because they
are not thinking for me. They taught me about Old King
Cole and Mary had a little lamb, it's fleece was white as
snow, and Bah Bah Black Sheep, the black death, cotton
mills and the industrial revolution. But they omitted to tell
me about slavery, the blood isn't on my hands.

What do you want me to do, live or die, or haven't you
thought about it? Is it just up to me, well let me see, I could
let the anger fester, start a riot every so often, mug you and
not know why, hate you blind and keep the fire burning.
Do you know how angry I am? I'm not going to ask you if
you care 'cause many of us have gone beyond that, and at
your ignorance suffered too much to listen anymore to
your deceit. What did I hear you say, I'm nothing to do
with you I'm not your business, I'm just something for you
to exercise your liberal conscience, God have mercy ... my
fathers gave you your wealth and position while you
whipped them and I have inherited the disadvantage while

you gloat like it's a natural thing. I'm not going to sit here and watch you. I'm going to take something if you don't give it to me.

Wait until judgement ... I'm not afraid to die.

My mother taught me everyone is equal, to love everyone and to say my prayers and go to Sunday school. While their mothers were telling them not to go near us, but I'm not quite sure why. They swing from trees or something. They might as well have said listen son, listen daughter, I don't know what's wrong with them but don't go near them anyway and meanwhile I'm going to think up the stupidest thing I can because we're just plain ignorant.

They told us we made no valuable contribution to this oh – so civilised world and we were running around naked when they found us. They didn't find us, they came looking for us. We never went looking for them. There was no need to! My father used to speak to me sometimes. He told me about the caveman and what colour he was so I could go to school armed with some return abuse. But it was as if I needed more. I needed to advance to realise and something was keeping me from that.

Then I discovered people, philosophers, black ones, musicians, black ones, sports men and women, black ones, inventors, black ones, scientists, black ones. The root of culture, civilisation began to materialise right in front of my eyes, as if some face from the past had meant me to know this. I could see nothing other than the words 'black', 'white' and 'conspiracy'.

VO/OLD WEST INDIAN MAN : Let me tell you someting young man. Look at yourself. Look back and look forward. To move on, right. To move on, listen me. It's a combination. Watch, listen, tink in a you head. Don't mek your mind so speedy. I'm coming from a long way and my father and his father before him are coming from even further. My son, take up de mantle and show dese man what you can do. Don't die under false oppression. Look back when you want to feel pain. Look forward when you want to feel joy. To all my son and to all my daughter, I love you you know. I really do and all those men and women really did love you too you know ... From Alexander Bustamante to Rosa Parks. They all cared to do dem lickle bit. Now, even if you tink, you, you know, not anybody else, you! You tink that I haven't done anyting for you, you'd be wrong because I've lived through it all and that living was for you.

YOUNG MAN: Old man, you know I'm just frustrated. I really feel robbed sometimes and when people say I've got it good, sometimes I just wanna fight and I don't wanna stop. I wonder man. I think about the past and it loses me and the future confuses me. But I hear what you say old man. You're saying I've got people. I've got people to support me, to take as an example, I know this. OK my don I'll have to find out who some of these people are so that I can use them. I know it wasn't just down to me. I know I had support somewhere.

I'll make a move, I'll keep on moving. I know what time it is. I'll take the knowledge and like my mum said, ask God for wisdom. I know there's people. Like Malcolm, Du Bois, Marley, Tubman, Baldwin, Benjamin Banneker and a whole heap of others. And I think there are still loads more out there somewhere. God, I could just do with speaking to them now. If I could just ask one question to each of them. But I'll tell you one thing my mother used to say, I never knew what she meant. But she said, "you should have an exodus, a return, in your mind and body, physically or mentally, to that place all Moors should go". And she taught me a poem of all impossible things and said these things are possible because they happen in the poem.

To himself at low volume.

One fine day in the middle of the night
Two dead men got up to fight
Two blind men to see the fun
One dumb man to shout hurrah
A paralysed donkey was passing by
Kick the blind man in his eye
Kicked him through a nine inch wall
And drowned him in a dry foot pan

Takes a coin out of his pocket and tosses it into the air, pronouncing the outcome before it lands.

Tails!

He heads towards off without checking to see if he's correct.

Tails it is!

Music Bob Marley's Exodus.

THE END

TO RAHTID

Author's Note

If you spoke everything you saw and felt for you and your ancestors, this is what you might say...

Sol B. River's 'To Rahtid'

To the family

Sometimes a writer can slip into some dangerous and easily misunderstood depths that are not always coherent. As a rule you cannot present none coherent work for obvious reasons. Within *To Rahtid* the none cohesion makes perfect sense, what doesn't make perfect sense is the calamitous situation that created that none cohesion and as a result the state of mind you will see in the text.

To Rahtid found its way into my mind by way of persistence. It was also to a certain extent already a part of my existence. There is no way that I can begin to feel the physical and psychological pain that my ancestors had to endure but I do feel the effects of the legacy and realise the evidence of it. This piece was painful to write, is painful to read and is probably quite painful to watch. I ask you to endure.

Sol B. River 1996

Foreword

Yvonne Brewster

What did these three pages of densely typed text mean? One way to delay facing the challenge was to challenge:

What did *To Raatid* mean?
Would you believe it?
Surely then that *To Raatid* had an h?
To Rahtid it became.
This was a genuine parody of Not I, was it?
Yes.

Once the delaying tactics were exhausted Angela Wynter (who was to perform the piece) and I asked Sol to read for us. As we sat through his whispered rendition we got the confidence to tackle *To Rahtid.* Some of the phrases were strange in the mouth. Was it written in English-Jamaican?

After a few minor idiomatic changes... prefer instead of favour, cut instead of trown, Sol went back to Leeds and we were on our own.

Angela and me. And three pages of densely typed text.

We found that although the text was not sequential there was a cry which linked and indicated the movement and changing thrusts of the piece.

Deal wid dis. Deal wid dis. Deal wid dis. Deal wid dis!

So using four different coloured markers we split up the text into its different rhythms and voice.

Green for Africa.
Pink for England
Yellow for Jamaica
Orange for Rebel England.

As we worked the piece and as Angela committed it to memory (a Herculean task) the images became clearer and more powerful in their simplicity. The clue was never to wonder why one had been so intimidated in the beginning. That was a sure way of losing it... to rahtid!

Yvonne Brewster 1996
Artistic Director of Talawa Theatre Company

Characters

MOUT

To Rahtid was first performed at the Young Vic Studio, London, on 22nd February 1996, with the following cast:

MOUT,   Angela Wynter

Direction,   Yvonne Brewster
Design,   Sue Mayes
Lighting,   John Linstrum
Sound,   Dan Lloyd

House lights come down to black. Silence. Sudden light to reveal the face of MOUT, the face of MOUT is surrounded by the light of a golden pyramid, every thing else remains in darkness. Right on the light MOUT begins to speak.

MOUT: ... move in a dis style ... dat style ... lickle pickney ting ... time soon come ... dear lord – ... but wait ... pickney gal? ... uh hu ... lickle pickney gal ... in an ... out in a ... time come too quick ... wretched hold ... name ... name ... never mine ... brethren forgotten ... long gone ... dem been punish ... tin air gone ... lickle after sun wake the day ... mother gone ... four hundred years duration ... not to de day ... love gone ... where de hope ... dem tek way de normal run ... hang de basket where we can't reach it ... held with a coffle ... in de hold ... no ... any and any punishment ... dem no love... until now noting ... you see you ... not a ting till de 50's when – ... kiss me neck back ... nineties? ... good lord! ... coming up two tousand... urban jungle... want for someting to make a reverse ... then lickle most ... look yonder ... move! ... lickle more ... lickle most again ... gawn ... we jus a drif ... it dawn pon me ... too late all de early life morning sun ... find demself ... wha dis? ... (*Kiss teeth.*) ... go way! ... dem! ... see dem in de hold ... mash up ... mad ... mad up ... de screaming piercing ... so it go ... in a de head ... orumila come and gone ... come and gone already ... like the sunset in Negril ... dipping in and out of sea ... but blood... seeing... me feel warm blood... never did know... where de compass did point ... deal wid dis ... de position in dat hold! ... stan up ... or die ... nough pain ... watch me now ... laying prostrate? ... listen me sir ... do I stan up?..stay laying... or... laying prostrate... nough pain... what? ... prostrate? ... yes sir ... don't stan up ... or sit down ... humility? ... adoration ... but nough pain still ... still ... never mine ... mi tink twice ... during an after ... sudden whip ... trust in gees u ... wid the master ... in a merciful ... (*Kiss teeth.*) ...Jesus... where arc you? ... tink tree times ... during an after ... sudden strike ... God did

punish us ... for ginalism ... ginal me? ... proof is proof
me need ... those who don't hear feel ... what me never
hear? ... during an after ... this foo foo ride ... it dawn on
me ... dem say ... it's OK ... deal wid dis! ... we is frien ...
mother land and ting ... offer-han ... shake ... but wait ... is
dis me is born for ... ha! ... the very tought ... dis time ...
in me life ... me should be drinking rum ... you know say
... me is having non ... not a taste ... so dat ... the whip
that inflic ... for noting ... or everting ... or noting ... dem
don't have no reason ... dem just favour it ... I overstand
... the whip that inflic ... me first did see it ... God believe
it ... be merciful... (*Kiss teeth.*) ... Jesus ... there is no Jesus
... it dawn on me... stupid ... foo foo ... no not foo foo ...
eh? ... uh uh ... give me a bligh ... what unu ... make me
tink ... big old whip ... stupid master ... what? ... me get
lick for dat ... turn dunce ... yes ... de screaming pearcing
... so it go ... in a de head ... in a me ear wax ... in a de
brain... chop like jelly coconut ... dis condition ... dash
my brain out ... full moon take place me head ... me turn
fool ... fool? ... nu mus ... pressure pon de chains dat hold
me ... sunrise ... sunset ... pressure pon de same place ...
where de rescue ... none ... part a dem plan ... torment ...
but wait... dem nu do dat ... no ... ha! ... me have a chance
... (*Kiss teeth.*) ... nu mus ... stop unu groaning ... what pain
... you must have a chip ... stop it! ... we can't ... someting
forever wrong ... me can't lie ... dem want me fi work
like a machine ... behave like a machine ... mud up ...
sack dat ... mi go fight you ... you hunt me ... make me
speak ... make me speak ... jus a word ... I beg una ...
make some noise ... bwoy bwoy bwoy ... listen me ... hu
hu hu hu ... again ... tek off de chain ... listen me again ...
... ... nuh ... spare noting ... as noisey as the dead in a
de bottom of the sea ... eh? ... de sailing? ... everyting
hush up except de waves ... we can't move ... that me
could feel ... just the coconut tree ... I tink ... dem could
see ... I could feel ... I did flex ... me nu move ... but de
trees ... dem have de best view ... swaying ... tilting ... all

that forsight because of dem height ... but me mind start
fi tinge ... eyes bigger than me belly ... oh yes ... me want
fi see ... everyting cool ... under manners ... what dis ... all
the early life morning sun ... de ship fix it eye ... I hear
someting ... dem come fi me ... de ship fix it eye ... you
see me all the light me ever had ... selfish ... but what dis
have to do with me ... oh ... new world what? ... me don't
have anyting fi you ... you want fi kill me ... bless dem at
the bottom of the sea ... me frighten ... uh uh ... it dawn
on me ... what? ... de language? ... yes ... all dead an daze
but for de language ... iron hot pon me ... language was ...
what? ... who dat? ... no ... dem! ... (*Kiss teeth.*) ... dawn on
me ... speech cut out of mout ... deal wid dis! ... orders a
come ... me no overstan ... listen me ... (*Whisper.*) ... de
sound constant ... de language it sounded ... me get fi
overstan ... dem give me basket fi carry water ... (*End
whisper.*) ... people jus a watch me ... me race ... it always
cole ... dem watch me freezing nu understanding ...
freezing bret ... slow bret ... we did never ... we can't
speak ... all dis time ... how me survive! ... urban life ... in
de town ... busy concrete jungle ... market ... list wat me
want ... yam, ackee, plantain ... big ol bag ... den me wait
... big length of time ... dem don't have what me want ...
turn dupy ... eyes turn big ... bottom lip drop ... big ol
bag full o potato ... full o potato ... den me gawn ... me
nu say ta ta ... how me can stan! ... and now freezing bret
... see me bret ... slower bret ... tink ... what is dis ... deal
wid dis! ... blaggage ... me nu feel so good ... mad is
crazy... not potato... where de yam?..me lip say... no yam
... vital food gone ... lickle most ... strive I strive ... I feel
... me feel ... I feel too ... deal wid dis ... mout quivering
... dem don't stand alone ... de special shaped skull ... mi
wide nose ... de whole face ... all dem ... feature ... warrior
feature ... the large lips? ...yes ... the large lips around the
mout ... dem features ... wid out dem ... no chat ... all dem
... features ... heritage ... history ... without dat no chat ...
no make me nu feel me features ... where dem gone ...

dem change me ... dem intent ... what me saying ... whole
ting gone bad ... hanging on a tred ... not only de features
... me had ... had me ... me taught did gone ... me voice
did weak ... during an after ... you want tin lips now? ...
sudden whip ... don't care how it is ... stomach feel bad ...
deal wid dis ... stomach bad ... start in hell ... work down
... de whole system ... stop dat ... dear lord ... de mout and
de mind ... see me ... me straining ... how long ... sudden
whip ... me can't stan it ... all dis ... all dat ... freezing
mout ... straining to overstan ... mek someting of it ... and
me tink mek someting of dis ... all dis ... eh? ... de
language ... uh hu ... all de time de language ... so call ...
all a de problem ... deal wid dis! ... whole history gone ...
you want tin lips ... angled cheeks ... soft jaw? ... never! ...
yes sir! ... what? ... feature warrior feature ... natty dread
ride again ... no problem ... mout on fire ... word catch
alight ... ear clear ... word in the mind ... in your ... me
speak to dem ... dem no understan ... not a quarter ... dem
hard ears ... deal wid dis ... can't stop me ... nu cease...
quite una ... hush up ... hush una self ... hear me now ...
stop it ... come now ... can't stop de shout ... me whole
body a go beg ... someting in me head ... beg una mout
to stop ... hush up ... dem a go kill you ... stop fly your
mout ... brain never stop ... it nu hear ... or refuse ... it
never stop ... it enfuse ... me no mad ... but the mind ...
me can't hear ... wait a little ... de mind ... jus a run ...
lickle at a time ... mind mi tell you ... you can't hear me?
... couldn't ... can't even pause ... hook up ... everyting
together ... strain me strain ... jigsaw me a put together ...
de mind ... life it have ... talk sense nu ... or stop your
noise ... dig up de pass ... dragg up de pass ... whip from
all over de place ... walk bare foot mostly ... walk never
ride ... century more century ... move then lickle most ...
look yonder ... step ... lickle more ... lickle most again we
jus a lost ... hold me head down ... tear jus a drop ... me
never cry ... since me was a pickney ... me cry like a
pickney ... no woman no cry ... me no cry ... stop dat ...

me no cry since me was a pickney ... crying ... me never
cry till ... life pass already ... coffle mark me neck back ...
where? ... Mo bay ... de inner city remind me ... de
hypocracy ... one night me did look ... on de way home
... home! ... where dat ... me see the night ... der in the
night ... in me mother lap ... suddenly saw the dead ... de
gone ... tears ... all dat crying ... me sit alone ... de tears ...
dem can't finish ... flex yourself ... no bother ... drip drip
... de mind still a go ... fine yourself ... hole on ... to
what? ... move on ... voice still bad ... dem say it mek no
sense ... everyting heavy ... is what? ... de language? ... uh
hu ... de language ... fall like Dunn's River ... and de sun
... rising and setting ... and it set in de north ... full moon
tek place me head ... try fi keep me eye open ... tird eye
... me can't go on ... Jah! ... me get dis ... back in de
jungle de concrete ... early life sun ... face down in de
ship ... noting but John Crow ... so it go ... waiting ...
hard ears ... one an two word ... make lickle sense ...
whole history in danger ... like de mout ... mad it mad ...
can't stop ... nough noise ... someting dem did ...
someting I have to ... who dat? ... no! ... dem! ... (*Kiss
teeth.*) ... I know what dem did ... what? ... I do ... de
language? ... uh hu ... all de time de language ... in a me
head ... and de sun ... rising around ... painless ... lie ... ha!
... dem tinking ... during and after ... sudden whip ...
could be ... dem did ... tell dem ... I have to ... tis
necessary ... tell ... lickle ting ... time soon come...
wretched hold ... dem nu love ... stop hope ... held me
talk ... how me did exist! ... the time dem capture ... what
you have fi say ... innocent ... harambe ... race ... act up
race ... how you can stand ... staring into noting? ... mout
drop ... wait for de jinx ... ginal tek you away ... dem cuff
on you han ... now den ... someting I have to ... could dat
be it? ... dat can tell ... de story ... how dem ... treat us ...
uh hu ... damage ... how we suffer ... it live ... own up ...
so it go ... to be ... de 50's ... dem ... yes! ... kiss me neck
back de nineties? ... dear Lord! coming up two tousand ...

you don't know ... if me nu tell you Jah love ... one love
... tender love him gi me ... early life morning sun ... sink
down in de ship ... de John Crow ... so it go ... hold your
head up ... move una self ... lickle more ... move! ... all
right ... another flex ... try another ting ... tink of next
flex ... during and after ... sudden whip ... another ting ...
no ... someting try another ting ... so it go ... soon come
... after a time ... tings forgiven ... tink back to ... what? ...
not dat ... noting to do wid dem ... noting me could
forgive – ... who dat? ... no! ... dem! ... (*Kiss teeth.*) ...
lickle pickney ting ... time come too quick ... wretched
hole ... love gone ... spared hope ... held with a coffle ...
held me talk ... even to me ... can't say noting loud ... is
me can't hold me ... a rush me get ... one and two lick ...
always cold ... strange ting ... dis long life ... night fall ...
get rush ... tell ... me run ... stop ... pour out me words ...
jus a run ... mad to de max ... words twiss up ... dem look
pon me ... me see dem fix gaze ... me move back ...
always cole ... night fall ... now dis ... dis ... more and
more ... de language ... de mind ... mad up flicker ... mek
me hole on ... to noting ... onto someting else ... all the
time me a pray ... someting praying ... pray it to stop ...
nu hear me ... Jesus nu hear me ... don't answer duppy
pray ... so it go ... move on ... try a ting ... if life spare ...
don't know ... what what me is trying? ... what to try ...
whole history could gone ... just like de mout ... like mad
up mud up ... so it go ... keep – ... what? ... de language ...
yes ... all de time de language ... fall like Dunn's River ...
in a me head and de sun ... bigging up ... pain me ... No!
... Dem! oh God! ... you know ... what me saying ... what
to do ... what me afer try ... no pay dem any mind ...
move on ... me know the truth ... forget the truth ... Jah is
love ... one love ... every life morning sun ... sink down
in de ship ... I see white John Crow ... dash it.

Sudden silence, MOUT bows slowly. Cut the light.

THE END

UNBROKEN

for

Phoenix Dance

Foreword

Thea Nerissa Barnes

I contacted Sol after reading articles in a publication called *Reading Bibles, Writing Bodies* (ed, Timothy K. Beal & David Gunn 1997). The articles explored how religion, political and cultural identities, including ethnicity and gender were embodied in the Book of Proverbs. For me the readings proved interesting subject matter with which to build a dance built on text. Since I wanted the text to have an afrocentric edge, I asked Sol if he could read the same articles in preparation for a script for either a male or female dancer.

In my estimation, dynamic tension is very important for a dance solo and the dialect, pitch and rhythm modulation between and within each of the monologues in Sol's script are important textures. The voices are male and female, old and young, familiar and foreign. The next texture is the sound of the different languages which are English, Jamaican Patois, Spanish, French and Portuguese. The next structural consideration for the dance is that the script is an episodic regarding a male and the choices he has made in relation to himself and his life. The female in this scenario is victim, martyr, heroine. For the dance, the script is the point of resonance because the interpretation can be from a male or female perspective. The dancer uses the script as an introspection for past experiences and imaginary future choices within an individual's journey. Whether this journey is through past, present or future life, or life at all, is left to the interpretation and contemplation of the dancer. The first day of rehearsal for the solo brought together four dancers; two female and two male. This day was spent reading and discussing the characters, perceived situations, and the meanings that each dancer got from the script. These discussions set the dance in the stage space and helped build the inner space that each dancer must create when performing the dance.

Unbroken the script will fuse with *Unbroken* the dance at the time of performance. The dancer, being either male or female, is the protagonist becoming and confronting issues and situations on a journey. The choreography is such that the script creates the environment in which the dance occurs or is the exact theme and rhythm upon which the dance moves. Contemporary dance is not always understood by audience members and perhaps this breakdown in communication is due to the nature of the dance. Dance is ephemeral, of the moment, and leaving images, perhaps some visceral sensing, maybe some small essence of recognised experience. Dance is not always tangibly explained or understood and even end of show conversations cannot reliably reveal what one has experienced.

Unbroken has been a challenge for all concerned; writer, dancer, choreographer, audience and I hope that at the point of performance all will sense the striving which the journey on stage portrays. Striving is common for all people and it is this universal essence that I hope will be seen. Essence is what is left as a source of contemplation 6 months to years after the performance is over and *Unbroken* has the potential of making this happen.

Thea Nerissa Barnes 1997
Artistic Director, Phoenix Dance Company

Characters

DANCER
FEMALE VOICE
MALE VOICE
OLD MAN
CHILD
NARRATOR
SPANISH VOICE
FRENCH VOICE
PORTUGUESE VOICE

Unbroken was first performed in the Royal Northern College of Music, Manchester, on 18 September 1997, with the following cast:

DANCER,	Booker T. Louis
Also performed by	Hugh Davis
	Seline Derrick
	Pamela L. Johnson

VOICES:

FEMALE VOICE (patois),	Angela Wynter
MALE VOICE (patois),	Wayne Buchanan
OLD MAN,	Joe Williams
CHILD,	Mica Derrick
NARRATOR,	Jhardine Farrell
SPANISH & FRENCH VOICES,	Karen Lopez
PORTUGUESE VOICE,	Luciana Lang

Choreographer,	Thea Nerissa Barnes
Technical Director,	Guy Dickens
Lighting Designer,	Spike Mosley

Author's note:

Unbroken was originally written to accomodate both a male and female dancing duet, or a male or female dancer dancing solo. Phoenix Dance Company's interpretation was to use one dancer at a time, either male or female.

The stage is black, we see nothing, then we see a fairy light lit structure of an outline of a harem that is centre stage The harem has gold and purple cushions in the centre of it and a sizeable silver dish of water from which the FEMALE DANCER can wash at various stages. We remain in darkness throughout the OLD MAN's introduction.

OLD MAN: The fear of the Lord is the beginning of knowledge; fools despise wisdom and instruction. Listen carefully to your father's instruction and don't reject your mother's teaching. If you see and know something is wrong don't follow it. If you join a bad crowd and they say come with us lie in wait for blood because they want to do some harm to some innocent person, don't join them. Walk on a different route.

NARRATOR: And when wisdom was realised it came in the shape and form of a feminine image, and a man witnessed this image in the flesh and was attracted to it. But the young man began to see the image as a threat because she was both beautiful and wise. And he became confused so that he disrespected and abused her and ignored his father's words and his mother's teaching ...

And so she was born innocent and in the flesh, wisdom that is, not knowing who she was. And he, the man, grew also.

The DANCERS enter during the text. Lights fade up to purple and blue and the moon appears in a star lit sky. The MALE DANCER throws sand into the Harem, the FEMALE DANCER throws petals. We hear a LITTLE GIRL's voice slightly echoed and distant coming through on top.

YOUNG FEMALE VO: When I grow up I want to love and I want to be loved.
Mummy said I should love God because
he is love.
Daddy didn't say anything because he isn't here.
I asked mummy if God was a man and she said

I'll tell you tomorrow.
I asked mummy if I was a good girl and
she said the smile in your eyes never lies.
I asked my mummy what God looked like
but she didn't know and nobody did.
My teacher at school learnt us about love
and I can spell it, I write about it all the time.
It was my first word.
I love love.
When I grow up I want to be it,
so I might learn how to be near to God.

It begins to snow. The MALE DANCER's movements excel better in this weather.

The following text is said in both male and female voices. Every so often the DANCERS lip-synch part of the text. In the recording of this text the whole piece should overlap itself and echo in its delivery.

MALE/FEMALE VO: Laugh, cry, lonely, can't get, dismiss, security, wonderful trip through our time, sing, hold me, cure me, cure you, cure me, vexation, imprecation, (*MAN.*) check, quash, subdue, stifle (*WOMEN.*) advance, animate, exhilarate (*MAN.*) and what does this mean? (*WOMEN.*) expedite, ascend, arise, assertion (*MAN.*) grasp, grip, bind, clutch, maintain, (*MAN & WOMEN.*) disorder, bewilder, displeasure, decrepit, disaster, no discipline, defamatory, disgrace, disconcerting, derogatory, distinction of the sign of the times. (*WOMEN.*) dwell in love, joy, peace, patience, kindness, goodness, faithfulness, gentleness, self control (*MAN.*) dwell in fornication, impurity, licentiousness, idolatry, sorcery, enmity, strife, jealousy, anger, selfishness, dissension, party spirit, envy, drunkenness, carousing and the like.

The snow has stopped, the sun begins to rise, colours change to gold and orange.

VO OLD MAN: The beginning of wisdom is this, get
wisdom but whatever you get, get understanding.

*During the following voice over the DANCERS begin to come
close but do not touch.*

FEMALE VO: If you could love like love intended,
love me, every part of me.
Know every inch of my soul,
don't try and take control,
hold my spirit while holding my hand
and the personification of each of our souls will enable
us to understand.

Si pudieras amar como el amor pretendia,
que ames cada parte de mi.
que conozcas profundamente mi alma,
no intentes apoderarte de mi,
sostén mi espíritu, al cogerme de la mano
y la personificación de cada una de nuestra almas nos
ayudará a entendernos.

Si tu pouvais aimer comme l'amour envisageait,
aimes-moi, chaque partie de moi.
Connais profondément mon âme,
ne tentes pas de me contrôler,
tiens mon esprit pendant que tu me tiens par la main
et la personnification de chacune de nos âmes nous
permettra de comprendre.

Se você pudesse amar como o amor pretendia,
que ame cada parte de mim
que conheça profundamente a minha alma
Não tente tomar controle
segure a minha alma, enquanto segura a minha mão
e a personificação de cada uma das nossas almas nos
ajudará a entender nos.

*The DANCERS are about to touch but the interruption of
the patois VOICE OVER causes them to part.*

FEMALE VO: When yuh llow dawg fi tase fowl egg, him
nyam de very shell all because him fool, pig neva know
the use a him tail till butcher chop it off because no care
how boar try fi hide under sheep wool him grunt always
betray him. Listen me sister is better fi lose yuh time dan
yuh character, stop it, come now, but I can't, nu yuh
mus, tell it, tell him how unu feel launch de appeal, cuss
du fake tings, yuh can have anyting you want in dis
world except cream nuh badda badda de badderation,
coming like omen, my man is no man, move way sister
him coming like pittar patter, when jackass back strong
dem overload her hamper, is what yuh do when yuh man
is untrue? Dat loving de loving dat everlasting love, me
want me man fi gi me but de impossibility de
promiscuous prolific can prolong it prolix. Is dis me
born for, move way, stop all dem, Talawa tings! Stop it,
come now, God is love, tender love him give me, Jah
love, one love, make me love him then, all my love to
my Jah, God is love, tender love him give me, no
women no cry over no man until man cry over me,
equilibrium tings you nu see, expect me to carry yuh
pickney me picky picky punni nu entry, not even for
company, heart break, love take, belly big an round, me
have fi spen de poun, man nu de round, fly in an out
when him belly hungry, lick me when im feel unhappy.
You want fi reck mi use mi crucify abuse me until my
mind's dispair and yuh nu want fi go there. Come on
stop it behave una self if you have it in you to love me
step back come forward an show me but as the Lord is
my God una will not use me.

Lighting turns a heavy blood red.

MALE VO: Watch mi, man nu dead, no call im duppy,
come here sweet bring de punni come on resist me
don't flex de face-ty firs come here and bear me a
pickney A my women dat, mi nu want fi abuse or use,
but de love disorder have de controller, as if me is

predestine to be a failure, my history disagree becau it deal wid royalty, but de social situation condones de frustration an I wallow in de damnation of myself. Mi love you you know, watch mi nuf gal but I going seccle. Sen it dem glorious pussy coming like dirt to royalty, mi han full can't manage numbers long like lottery, caramel, cream, plain chocolate an dem brownin tings from one to another like being in Narnia. Mi's a don wearing Gucci an Armani dollars falling out de mercede. Start it! Watch mi! smile an stride big up mi pride, ego going flow, ladies from head to toe, inspiration coming like desire, lower parts on fire, can't hold back de addiction for de duration falling into de casket every promise fit, juices like Niagara, flowing like Dunn's river. Kisses sweeter than a Rolex, to your body mines has to flex. Start dem! She loves, I can't spell it, break her heart, you want mi fi regret it? Mi want dat boopsie, when she smile in your eye then come de demise, the man in de moon is smiling im no what I is tinking, speedy love, fast love, bus a nut, come an love, then get back before she attach, like strap to mi back, want to seccle but de psychological babble riding on Robert Palmers saddle, addicted to love, like some hard drug, decease don't bother mi, daze an confuse me mus be bemuse, like dem string in a orchestra I'll continually play her, watch mi, crave mi, desire mi, want mi, carnal mi, stop mi, hold mi, lust mi, nu badda hide from mi all I want is yu ... crazy mi, irate mi, lunatic mi, demented mi, eh! a wa du yu is bandooloo? Bob an weave an de women still want me, buguyaga don't come straight Gaad at me gate but me still nu fraid. Devil await mi life gwaan speedy, cu-ya telling don dat hell looks on. Watch mi!

Mirrors are descending on to the stage, one for each DANCER, the DANCERS move in front of them with movements that represent their individual feelings.

Lights turn blue and orange for the following with both the sun and the moon in the sky at once.

FEMALE VO: If you open your heart, open your mind
　　　beat the drum, gaze the gaze, sing the song.
　　　Majestic openness, omnipotent truth,
　　　godliness shining, prejudice forbidden,
　　　floating in sun shine, shaking hands with the moon,
　　　listening to the water, drinking fresh rain dew,
　　　talking with the forest, rolling in the sand,
　　　listen to me my potential gentleman.
　　　Wishing is easy just say you believe
　　　nobody said love was stronger than you,
　　　there is a place I know, all the way in my heart
　　　profound inner peace, everlasting contract.
　　　Sitting down devouring the goodness of happiness.
　　　Just love, just peace, just feast, just embrace
　　　the park in your heart, pride in your mind, wishful
　　　thinking, truth everlasting.
　　　Rescued mission of love.

MALE VO: For the first time I've felt your beauty,
　　　for the first time I've caught your smile,
　　　the rain washed me dirty, the sun sticky
　　　but the moon shone on me repeatedly.
　　　I can't erase the love you placed,
　　　as strong as life itself.
　　　The love and respect of God is what I'm missing
　　　Stay and teach me if wishing is easy,
　　　plant me in your soul.
　　　I know I tried to break your heart
　　　but I broke my own gazing into a superficial zone,
　　　from here on I promise God takes control.

NARRATOR: And so it was that he began to arrive at the
　　　understanding of his mother's teaching and that the
　　　values of man were built into the structures of the world
　　　but his mother's values were built into the structures of
　　　his heart which contain his soul and his soul lives

forever. And she, that is wisdom and love, continued to fly and glide and teach those that would abuse her and her daughters because she was next to God since many had long since departed.

THE END